This Book Belongs To:

____

____

KINDERGARTEN

Practice! Color, trace, and then write the sight word.

all

Write a sentense using the word
and draw a picture above

Congratulations on your good work

KINDERGARTEN

Practice! Color, trace, and then write the sight word.

am

Write a sentense using the word
and draw a picture above

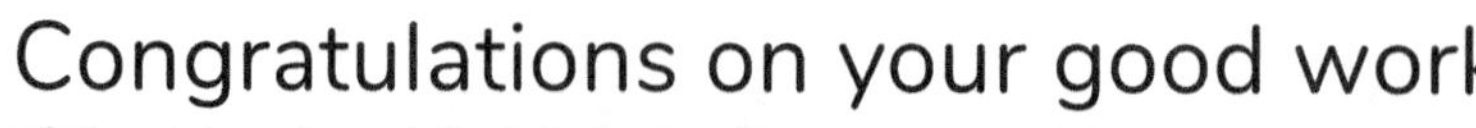

Congratulations on your good work

KINDERGARTEN

Practice! Color, trace, and then write the sight word.

are

 Write a sentense using the word
and draw a picture above 

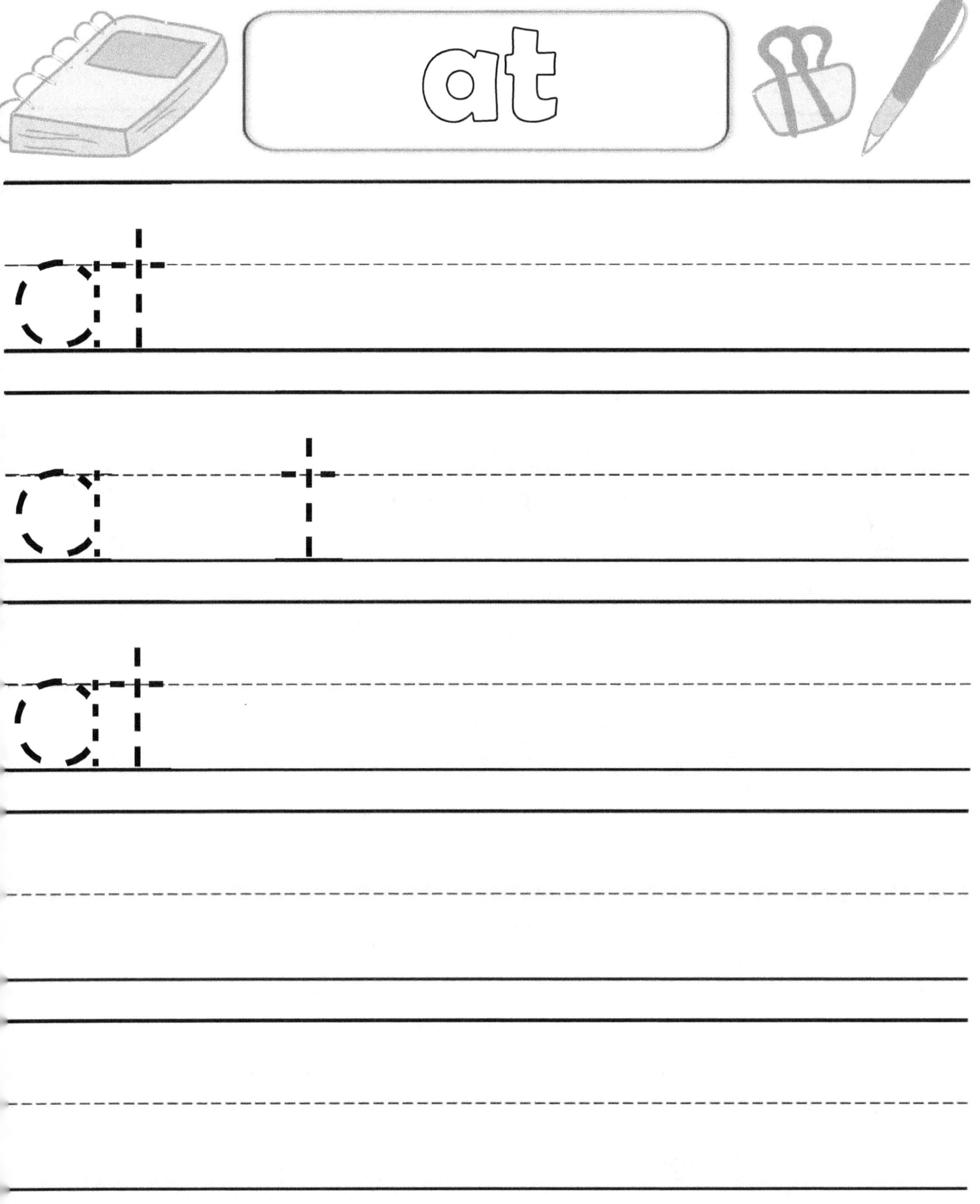

KINDERGARTEN

Practice! Color, trace, and then write the sight word.

at

Write a sentense using the word
and draw a picture above

 Congratulations on your good work 

KINDERGARTEN

Practice! Color, trace, and then write the sight word.

ate

 Write a sentense using the word
and draw a picture above 

 Congratulations on your good work 

KINDERGARTEN

Practice! Color, trace, and then write the sight word.

be

Write a sentense using the word
and draw a picture above

Congratulations on your good work

KINDERGARTEN

Practice! Color, trace, and then write the sight word.

black

Write a sentence using the word
and draw a picture above

Congratulations on your good work

KINDERGARTEN

Practice! Color, trace, and then write the sight word.

brown

Write a sentence using the word
and draw a picture above

 Congratulations on your good work 

KINDERGARTEN

Practice! Color, trace, and then write the sight word.

but

Write a sentense using the word
and draw a picture above

 Congratulations on your good work 

KINDERGARTEN

Practice! Color, trace, and then write the sight word.

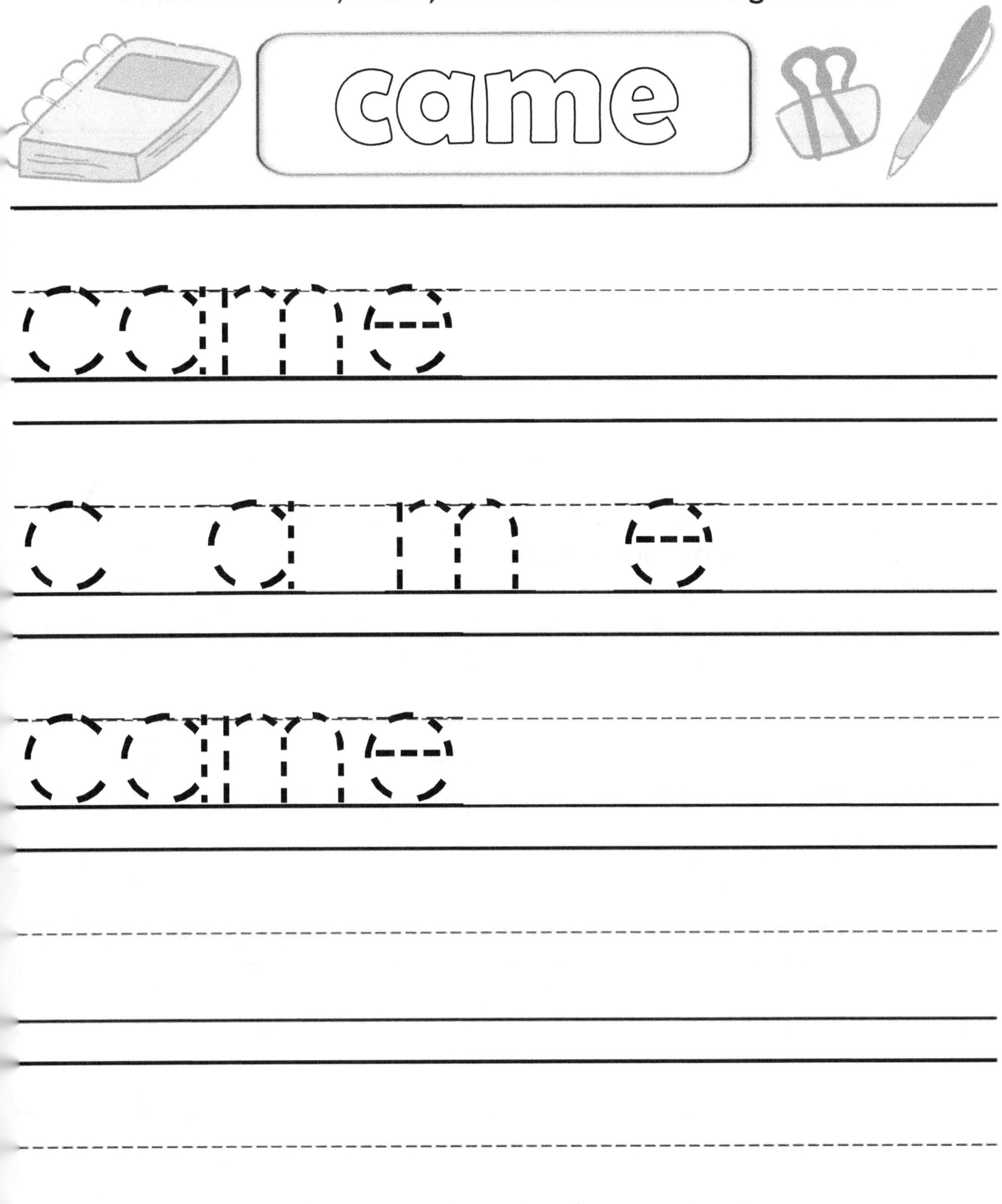

came

Write a sentense using the word
and draw a picture above

 Congratulations on your good work 

KINDERGARTEN

Practice! Color, trace, and then write the sight word.

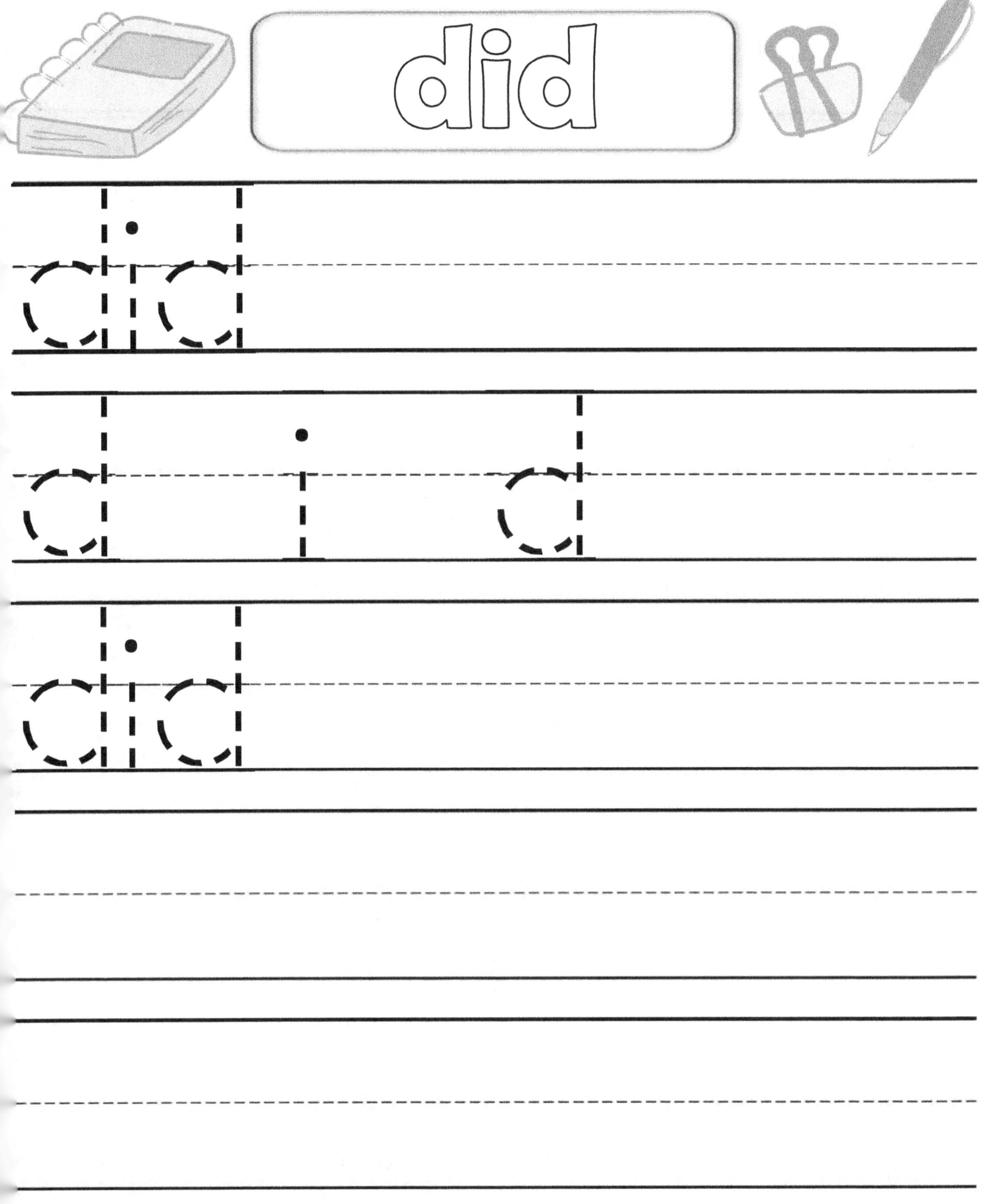

dib

Write a sentense using the word
and draw a picture above

 **Congratulations on your good work** 

KINDERGARTEN

Practice! Color, trace, and then write the sight word.

do

Write a sentense using the word
and draw a picture above

Congratulations on your good work

KINDERGARTEN

Practice! Color, trace, and then write the sight word.

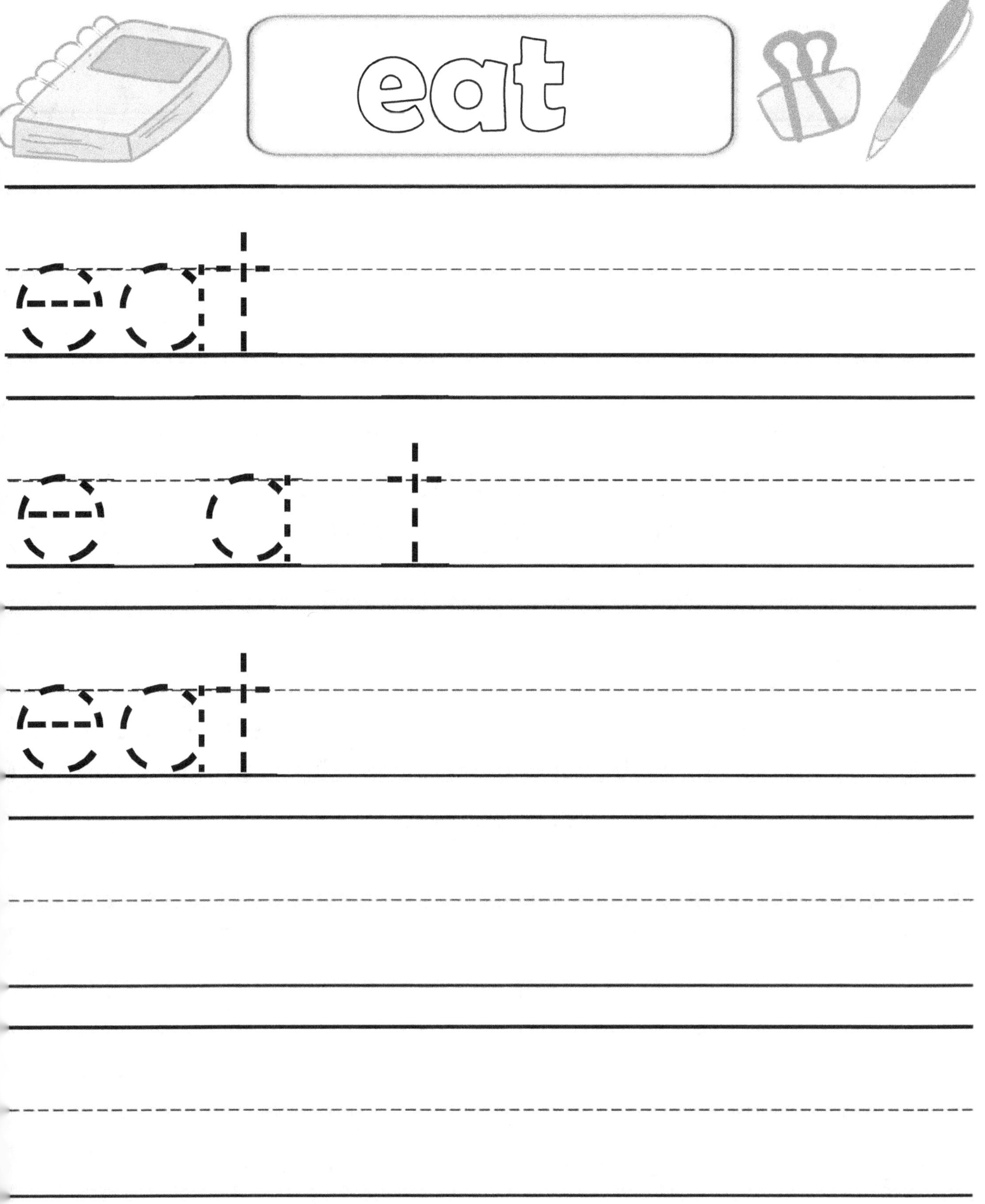

eat

Write a sentense using the word
and draw a picture above

 Congratulations on your good work 

KINDERGARTEN

Practice! Color, trace, and then write the sight word.

four

Write a sentense using the word
and draw a picture above

 Congratulations on your good work 

KINDERGARTEN

Practice! Color, trace, and then write the sight word.

get

Write a sentense using the word
and draw a picture above

 Congratulations on your good work 

KINDERGARTEN

Practice! Color, trace, and then write the sight word.

good

Write a sentense using the word
and draw a picture above

 Congratulations on your good work 

KINDERGARTEN

Practice! Color, trace, and then write the sight word.

have

Write a sentense using the word
and draw a picture above

 Congratulations on your good work 

KINDERGARTEN

Practice! Color, trace, and then write the sight word.

he

Write a sentense using the word
and draw a picture above

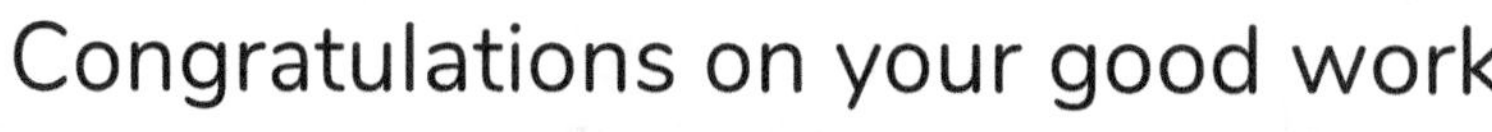

Congratulations on your good work

KINDERGARTEN

Practice! Color, trace, and then write the sight word.

into

Write a sentense using the word
and draw a picture above

Congratulations on your good work

KINDERGARTEN

Practice! Color, trace, and then write the sight word.

like

Write a sentense using the word
and draw a picture above

 Congratulations on your good work 

KINDERGARTEN

Practice! Color, trace, and then write the sight word.

must

Write a sentence using the word
and draw a picture above

Congratulations on your good work

KINDERGARTEN

Practice! Color, trace, and then write the sight word.

new

Write a sentense using the word
and draw a picture above

 Congratulations on your good work 

KINDERGARTEN

Practice! Color, trace, and then write the sight word.

no

Write a sentense using the word
and draw a picture above

Congratulations on your good work

KINDERGARTEN

Practice! Color, trace, and then write the sight word.

now

Write a sentense using the word
and draw a picture above

Congratulations on your good work

KINDERGARTEN

Practice! Color, trace, and then write the sight word.

on

Write a sentense using the word
and draw a picture above

 Congratulations on your good work 

KINDERGARTEN

Practice! Color, trace, and then write the sight word.

our

Write a sentense using the word
and draw a picture above

Congratulations on your good work

KINDERGARTEN

Practice! Color, trace, and then write the sight word.

out

Write a sentense using the word
and draw a picture above

 Congratulations on your good work 

KINDERGARTEN

Practice! Color, trace, and then write the sight word.

please

Write a sentense using the word
and draw a picture above

 Congratulations on your good work 

KINDERGARTEN

Practice! Color, trace, and then write the sight word.

pretty

Write a sentense using the word
and draw a picture above

Congratulations on your good work

KINDERGARTEN

Practice! Color, trace, and then write the sight word.

ran

Write a sentense using the word
and draw a picture above

Congratulations on your good work

KINDERGARTEN

Practice! Color, trace, and then write the sight word.

ride

Write a sentence using the word
and draw a picture above

 Congratulations on your good work 

KINDERGARTEN

Practice! Color, trace, and then write the sight word.

saw

Write a sentense using the word
and draw a picture above

Congratulations on your good work

KINDERGARTEN

Practice! Color, trace, and then write the sight word.

say

Write a sentense using the word
and draw a picture above

 Congratulations on your good work 

KINDERGARTEN

Practice! Color, trace, and then write the sight word.

she

Write a sentense using the word
and draw a picture above

 Congratulations on your good work 

KINDERGARTEN

Practice! Color, trace, and then write the sight word.

SO

Write a sentense using the word
and draw a picture above

Congratulations on your good work

KINDERGARTEN
Practice! Color, trace, and then write the sight word.
soon

soon

Write a sentense using the word
and draw a picture above

Congratulations on your good work

KINDERGARTEN

Practice! Color, trace, and then write the sight word.

that

Write a sentense using the word
and draw a picture above

 Congratulations on your good work 

KINDERGARTEN

Practice! Color, trace, and then write the sight word.

there

Write a sentense using the word
and draw a picture above

 Congratulations on your good work 

KINDERGARTEN

Practice! Color, trace, and then write the sight word.

they

Write a sentense using the word
and draw a picture above

 Congratulations on your good work 

KINDERGARTEN

Practice! Color, trace, and then write the sight word.

this

Write a sentense using the word
and draw a picture above

 Congratulations on your good work 

KINDERGARTEN

Practice! Color, trace, and then write the sight word.

too

Write a sentense using the word
and draw a picture above

 Congratulations on your good work 

KINDERGARTEN

Practice! Color, trace, and then write the sight word.

under

Write a sentense using the word
and draw a picture above

 Congratulations on your good work 

KINDERGARTEN

Practice! Color, trace, and then write the sight word.

want

Write a sentense using the word
and draw a picture above

 Congratulations on your good work 

KINDERGARTEN

Practice! Color, trace, and then write the sight word.

was

Write a sentense using the word
and draw a picture above

 Congratulations on your good work 

KINDERGARTEN

Practice! Color, trace, and then write the sight word.

well

Write a sentense using the word
and draw a picture above

 Congratulations on your good work 

KINDERGARTEN

Practice! Color, trace, and then write the sight word.

went

Write a sentense using the word
and draw a picture above

Congratulations on your good work

KINDERGARTEN

Practice! Color, trace, and then write the sight word.

what

Write a sentense using the word
and draw a picture above

 Congratulations on your good work 

KINDERGARTEN

Practice! Color, trace, and then write the sight word.

white

Write a sentense using the word
and draw a picture above

 **Congratulations on your good work** 

KINDERGARTEN

Practice! Color, trace, and then write the sight word.

who

Write a sentense using the word
and draw a picture above

 Congratulations on your good work 

KINDERGARTEN

Practice! Color, trace, and then write the sight word.

will

Write a sentense using the word
and draw a picture above

 Congratulations on your good work 

KINDERGARTEN

Practice! Color, trace, and then write the sight word.

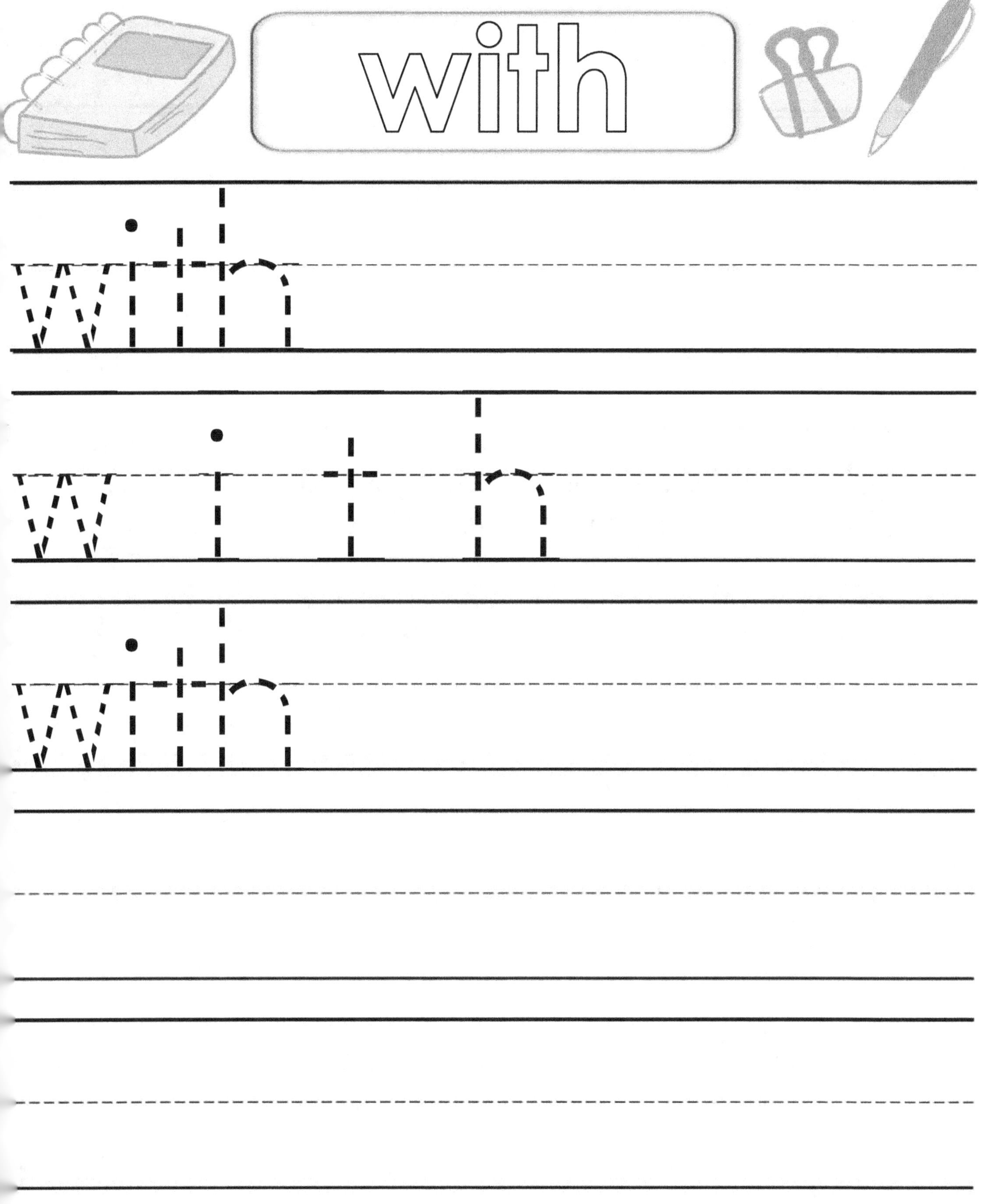

with

Write a sentense using the word
and draw a picture above

 Congratulations on your good work 

KINDERGARTEN

Practice! Color, trace, and then write the sight word.

yes

Write a sentense using the word
and draw a picture above

 Congratulations on your good work 

Kindergarten Sight Words

all	but
am	came
are	did
at	do
ate	eat
be	four
black	get
brown	good

Kindergarten Sight Words

have

he

into

like

must

new

no

my

now

on

our

out

please

pretty

ran

ride

Kindergarten Sight Words

saw	this
say	too
she	under
so	want
soon	was
that	well
there	went
they	what

Kindergarten Sight Words

white	
who	day
will	other
with	part
yes	people
	long
	her
	his